MW01538062

CROWN OF SUCCESS

Spells and Rituals to Manifest Wealth and Abundance

Jenny Andrieux

CONTENTS

INTRODUCTION
MANIFESTING ABUNDANCE THROUGH THE POWER OF NATURE

For centuries, people have turned to the wisdom of herbs, spices, and natural elements to influence the energies around them, attracting wealth and abundance into their lives. The energy of money is a force that can be harnessed, and in this book, I will share with you simple yet potent rituals that tap into this energy to help manifest prosperity, success, and financial freedom.

But remember, as the Bible says,

"Prayer without work is dead."

Manifesting money is not about waiting for a windfall to appear out of nowhere. It is about aligning your energy with the universe and putting forth the effort to see results.

You must plant the seed—set the intention—and take inspired action towards your goals. The money may come in many forms:

A gift, a new job opportunity, a bonus from work, or an unexpected windfall. The key is to open yourself to receiving in any form that presents itself.

This book is here to guide you in using herbs, spices, and the elements to amplify your efforts. These natural tools serve as conduits, helping to shift energy and attract the financial blessings you deserve. By performing these rituals with intention and faith, you'll learn how to ease the path to manifesting money and make it a natural part of your life. Let this journey be a powerful catalyst in turning your dreams of financial abundance into reality.

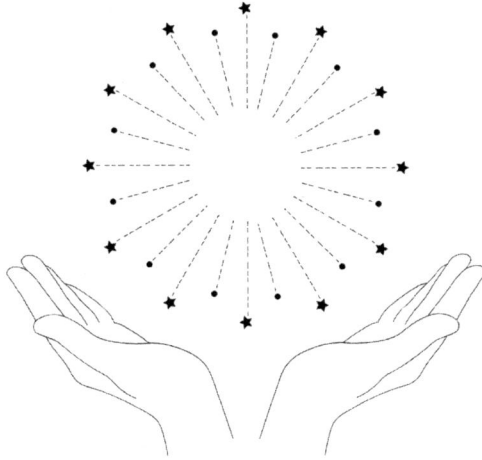

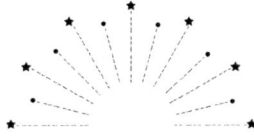

01

THE MAGIC OF TIMING AND TOOLS IN MONEY WORK

W hen it comes to manifesting prosperity and abundance, the timing and tools you choose play a significant role in enhancing the potency of your spells and rituals. The universe is full of cosmic rhythms, and each day of the week is governed by a different planet, influencing various aspects of life, including wealth and prosperity. Understanding which days and elements to work with can help align your intentions with the natural flow of energy, amplifying the results of your efforts.

THE DAYS OF THE WEEK AND THEIR PLANETARY INFLUENCE

Each day of the week is connected to a planet that governs specific aspects of our lives. For money and prosperity work, certain days are more potent than others:

Monday (Moon): The Moon governs intuition, emotions, and the flow of wealth. It is a good day for setting intentions related to new beginnings, emotional clarity, and nurturing the flow of money into your life.

Thursday (Jupiter): Jupiter is the planet of abundance, prosperity, and expansion. It is by far the most powerful day for doing money work. On Thursdays, the energy is aligned perfectly for growth, financial opportunities, and long-term wealth. This is the day to perform your most significant prosperity spells.

Sunday (Sun): The Sun rules over success, vitality, and recognition. It is an excellent day to perform rituals that focus on career growth, increasing visibility, and drawing attention to your financial talents and efforts.

THE POWER OF CANDLE COLORS IN MONEY WORK

Candles are a powerful tool in any spell, as their flame represents the manifestation of intention. For money work, certain colors of candles help direct the energy toward your specific goals:

Green: The color of abundance, wealth, and growth. Green candles are ideal for spells that focus on attracting money, prosperity, and success.

Gold: A symbol of wealth, luxury, and financial power. Gold candles are perfect for rituals designed to bring in wealth and increase your material fortune.

Silver: Silver is associated with the flow of money, especially for those looking to bring in unexpected financial opportunities or enhance their financial luck.

White: White is a versatile color that represents purity, clarity, and spiritual alignment. It can be used to amplify all types of money work, creating a strong foundation for your intentions and enhancing the energy of your spells.

AMPLIFYING YOUR MAGIC WITH HERBS AND OILS

The power of herbs and oils cannot be underestimated in magical work. These natural elements carry their own energies, and when used correctly, they can significantly amplify your spells. When working on money magic, the right combination of herbs and oils can align your energy with your desires and increase the chances of success.

Cinnamon: Known for its association with prosperity, abundance, and quick financial gain, cinnamon is an excellent herb to use in money spells. It can be sprinkled on candles or added to money-drawing sachets.

Basil: A herb of good fortune and wealth. Basil is often used to attract abundance and remove financial obstacles. You can use fresh or dried basil in your rituals.

Patchouli: A powerful herb for attracting wealth, success, and material gain. Patchouli can be used as an oil, in incense, or as a dried herb in sachets or candles.

Mint: Mint is a powerful herb for money work, known for drawing wealth and financial opportunities. Use it in spells focused on growth and increased income.

Money-Drawing Oil: A blend of essential oils, including cinnamon, ginger, and patchouli, money-drawing oil can be used to anoint candles, your hands, or your money altar to attract wealth.

By carefully selecting the right herbs and oils, you are not just adding a magical element to your ritual; you are tapping into the natural energy they bring to the work. They complement the energy of the day and enhance the overall flow of your intention, giving your spell more of a chance to succeed.

ALIGNING WITH THE UNIVERSE

When you align your work with the natural rhythms of the universe—through the right timing, colors, and tools—you are sending a clear and powerful message to the universe about your intentions. By using the energy of the planets, the colors of the candles, and the essence of herbs and oils, you enhance the effectiveness of your magic, making your path to prosperity smoother and more direct.

As you begin your journey into the world of money magic, keep these practices in mind. The universe is always working with you, but you must learn how to harness that energy and direct it toward your desires. With the right knowledge, focus, and intention, prosperity and abundance are within your reach.

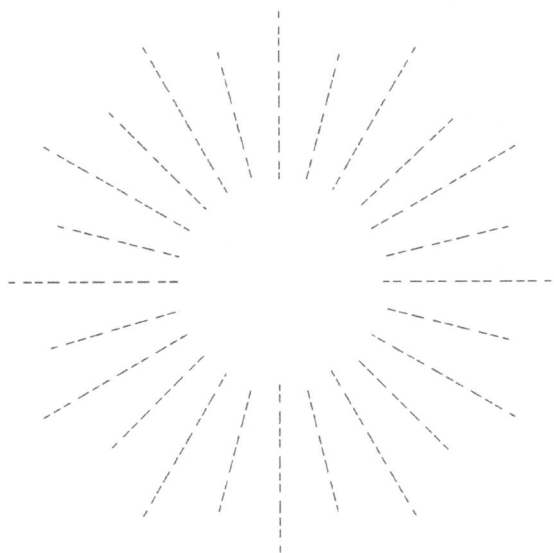

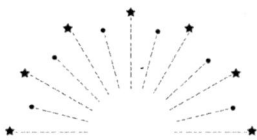

02

SIMPLE PROSPERITY SPELL FOR A NEW JOB

❦

*T*his spell is designed to attract new career opportunities into your life, whether you're looking for a full-time position, a side hustle, or any new professional opportunity.

WHAT YOU'LL NEED:

- A green candle (for abundance and growth) A yellow candle (for success and personal power)
- A piece of paper and a pen
- A small dish or bowl of salt (for purification)
- A few sprigs of basil (for good fortune and prosperity)
- A small amount of money (any denomination)
- A piece of clear quartz (to amplify the energy)
- A comfortable, quiet space

INSTRUCTIONS:

1. Prepare Your Space: Find a quiet space where you won't be disturbed. Set up your candles by placing the green one on your left (to symbolize attracting opportunities) and the yellow one on your right (to symbolize personal success). Place the small dish of salt in front of you for purification, and scatter a few sprigs of basil around the candles for added good fortune.

2. Focus Your Intentions: Sit quietly and center yourself. Close your eyes and take a few deep breaths to relax. Picture yourself in your ideal job, happy and successful. Feel the emotions of landing your dream position—pride, excitement, peace.

3. Write Your Intention: On the piece of paper, write down your job goal in the present tense, as if you've already received the job. For example: "I have found a fulfilling, rewarding job that brings me success and abundance."

4. Light the Candles: Light the green and yellow candles, focusing on the flames and your job intentions. Visualize these flames drawing positive energy and new opportunities toward you. Hold the clear quartz in your hands and feel its energy amplifying your wishes.

5. Charge Your Paper: Hold the paper with your job intention over the flames (but not too close) for a few seconds, letting the energy of the candles charge it. Imagine the energy of the candles activating your written intention.

6. Burn the Paper (Optional): If you wish, you can burn the paper in the candle flames (safely) as a symbolic gesture of releasing your intention into the universe. If you're not comfortable with burning it, simply fold it and place it under the small money (which represents abundance) on your altar.

7. Final Affirmation: Hold the piece of money in your hand and say aloud:

> *"I call forth the perfect job, Prosperity and success will flow, With every step, my path will grow, Abundance is mine, I claim it now."*

8. Close the Ritual: Once you've completed the affirmation, leave the candles to burn down safely. Keep the small piece of money with you, either in your wallet or your workspace, as a reminder of the abundance you're attracting. You can also carry the clear quartz with you to amplify the energy.

Note: Be open to new opportunities and take action when they arise. The spell works best when you align your energy with real-world efforts—apply for jobs, network, and stay positive.

This simple yet powerful spell helps focus your energy on attracting a new job, with the added strength of the candles, herbs, and your clear intention.

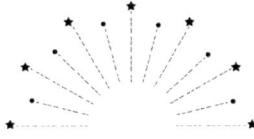

03

SIMPLE ROAD-OPENER SPELL

his road-opener spell is designed to help remove obstacles and clear the path for new opportunities in any area of your life. It's simple, but when performed with clear intention, it can be very effective.

BEST DAY TO PERFORM THIS SPELL:

Thursday (Jupiter): Thursday is the day of Jupiter, the planet of expansion and abundance, making it the best day for clearing roadblocks and inviting prosperity and growth.

BEST MOON PHASE:

Waxing Moon: The Waxing Moon is the phase when the moon is growing in strength, symbolizing expansion, new beginnings, and the clearing of obstacles. This phase is perfect for manifesting new opportunities and breaking down barriers in your path.

WHAT YOU'LL NEED:

- A green candle (for prosperity and new opportunities)
- A black candle (for removing obstacles)
- A piece of paper and a pen
- A small dish of water (for emotional flow and openness)
- A pinch of sea salt (for protection)
- A small amount of road-opening oil (or a mixture of cinnamon, ginger, and frankincense oils)
- A comfortable, quiet space

INSTRUCTIONS:

1. Prepare Your Space: Choose a quiet space where you will not be disturbed. Place the green candle on your left (for attracting opportunities) and the black candle on your right (for clearing obstacles). Place a small dish of water in front of you and sprinkle a pinch of sea salt around your candles to create a protective circle.

2. Set Your Intentions: Sit comfortably, close your eyes, and take a few deep breaths to center yourself. Focus on any obstacles or challenges you are facing and visualize them dissolving, making way for smooth, open roads filled with opportunity.

3. Light the Candles: Light the black candle first, saying:

"Obstacles vanish, barriers fall, The path is open, I hear the call."

Then light the green candle, saying:
"New opportunities, come to me, The road is clear, I am free."

4. Write Your Intention: On the piece of paper, write down what roadblocks you wish to remove and what new opportunities you are inviting. Be clear and concise. For example:

"I open the road to financial abundance, career growth, and success without hindrances."

5. Anoint the Paper: Dab the road-opening oil (or your essential oil mixture) onto the paper where you wrote your intention. Fold the paper toward you three times, symbolizing bringing opportunities and solutions into your life.

6. Place the Paper in the Water: Place the folded paper in the dish of water, symbolizing the flow of opportunities coming to you. Let the paper soak for a few minutes as you focus on your goal.

7. Final Affirmation: After the paper has soaked, remove it from the water, and say aloud:

"The road is clear, the path is wide,
Opportunities flow from every side.
I welcome abundance, I welcome ease,
All blockages are gone, my way is free."

8. Dispose of the Paper: Safely dispose of the paper, either by burying it or letting it burn (if done safely). As you do this, imagine the obstacles being completely cleared away from your path.

9. Close the Ritual: Leave the candles to burn down safely, and carry the energy of the ritual with you as you step forward into your day. You can keep the dish of water as a symbol of the flow of opportunities.

This road-opener spell, performed on a Thursday during the Waxing Moon, helps to clear obstacles and invite fresh, prosperous opportunities into your life. Use it as a tool to unblock your path, and remain open to the new doors that are about to open for you.

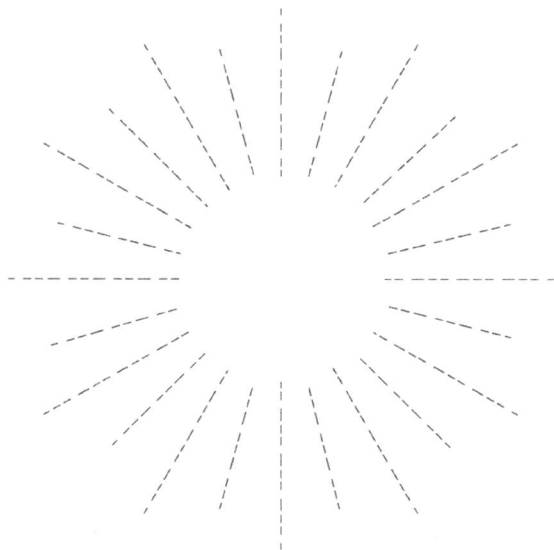

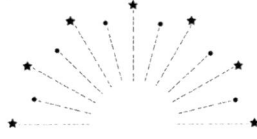

04

POWERFUL SPELL FOR QUICK MONEY

This spell is designed to attract quick financial gain and opportunities. It harnesses the energies of abundance and speed, drawing money into your life in a short amount of time.

BEST DAY TO PERFORM THIS SPELL:

Thursday (Jupiter): Jupiter is the planet of prosperity, abundance, and quick growth. Thursday is the best day to perform spells to draw quick money and increase financial opportunities.

BEST MOON PHASE:

Full Moon: The Full Moon is a powerful time for manifestation and bringing desires into fruition quickly. It amplifies your intentions and draws energy from the universe, making it an ideal time for attracting fast financial success.

WHAT YOU'LL NEED:

- A green candle (for abundance and wealth)
- A gold candle (for attracting quick money and success)
- A piece of paper and a pen
- A small dish of honey (for sweetening your financial opportunities)
- A pinch of cinnamon (for speed and financial attraction)
- A few coins (representing money flow)
- A small piece of citrine or pyrite (to attract wealth and success)
- A comfortable, quiet space

INSTRUCTIONS:

1. Prepare Your Space: Find a quiet, private space where you will not be disturbed. Place the green candle on your left (to attract wealth) and the gold candle on your right (to bring in fast financial gain). Set the dish of honey in front of you as a symbol of sweetening your financial flow. Place the coins around the candles and the citrine or pyrite next to the honey.

2. Set Your Intentions: Sit in a comfortable position and close your eyes. Take a few deep breaths to center yourself. Visualize money flowing into your life quickly, easily, and effortlessly. See yourself receiving unexpected financial gains—whether it's a gift, a bonus, or an opportunity that leads to fast wealth.

3. Light the Candles: Begin by lighting the green candle and say:

"Money flows easily, wealth is near, I welcome abundance, quick and clear."

Then, light the gold candle and say:

"l draw wealth, swift and bright, Fast money comes to me tonight."

4. Write Your Intention: On the piece of paper, write down the amount of money you desire and how you want it to come to you. Be specific and clear about your intention. For example:

"l attract $500 through unexpected opportunities, now and with ease."

5. Anoint the Paper: Dab a small amount of honey onto the paper, symbolizing the sweetness of financial gain. Sprinkle a pinch of cinnamon on the paper to bring speed and magnetism to your money draw.

6. Place the Coins on the Paper: Place the coins on top of the paper as a symbol of attracting financial flow. Let the energy of the coins amplify the intention to bring quick money into your life.

7. Hold the Citrine/Pyrite: Hold the citrine or pyrite in your hands. These stones are known for their ability to attract wealth and amplify energy. Close your eyes and focus on your intention while holding the stone. Visualize the money you seek coming to you in a quick, steady flow.

8. Final Affirmation: Hold the paper, coins, and stone in your hands and say aloud:

"I call upon the universe to bring, Quick money now, as I begin. Wealth flows swiftly, fast and true, The riches I seek are coming through."

9. Burn the Paper: Safely burn the paper in the flame of the candles, symbolizing the release of your intention into the universe. Allow the paper to burn completely, knowing that your request has been sent out.

10. Close the Ritual: Leave the candles to burn down completely. Keep the coins and citrine/pyrite with you as a reminder of the money you are attracting. Carry the energy with you, staying open to quick financial opportunities that come your way.

> **Note:** Keep an open mind and be ready to act on any unexpected opportunities that come your way. The universe works in mysterious ways, and sometimes money can flow through creative or surprising channels.

This powerful spell, performed during the Full Moon on a Thursday, helps draw fast financial gains and opportunities, aligning your energy with abundance and prosperity.

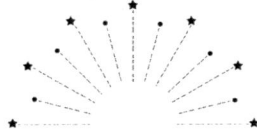

05

EASY AND POWERFUL SPELL TO WIN A GAME OF CHANCE

his spell is designed to enhance your luck and increase your chances of winning when participating in games of chance, like lotteries, raffles, or any other form of gambling.

BEST DAY TO PERFORM THIS SPELL:

Thursday (Jupiter): Jupiter is the planet of good fortune, luck, and expansion. Thursday is the best day to perform spells that boost luck and increase your chances of success in any game of chance.

BEST MOON PHASE:

Waning Moon: The Waning Moon is ideal for removing negativity and any blocks to your luck, allowing the energy to shift in your favor. This phase helps clear away any hindrances and lets positive luck flow to you.

WHAT YOU'LL NEED:

- A green candle (for good fortune and luck)
- A yellow candle (for success and personal power)
- A coin (representing chance and luck)
- A small dish of cinnamon (for attraction and speed)
- A small piece of clear quartz (to amplify the energy)
- A comfortable, quiet space

INSTRUCTIONS:

1. Prepare Your Space: Find a quiet, private space where you can focus without distractions. Place the green candle on your left (to attract luck) and the yellow candle on your right (for success and personal power). Set the small dish of cinnamon in front of you as a symbol of attracting luck and speed.

2. Set Your Intention: Sit in a comfortable position and take a few deep breaths to clear your mind. Focus on the game of chance that you are participating in, and visualize yourself winning. Imagine the feeling of success, excitement, and joy as you win the game. Feel the energy of luck on your side.

3. Light the Candles: Light the green candle first, saying:

"Luck is on my side, chance is mine, I draw good fortune, all will align."

Then, light the yellow candle, saying:

"Success and power, I now claim, Victory in the game, I win the name."

4. Hold the Coin: Take the coin in your hand and hold it between your palms. As you do so, visualize the coin shining with energy and your luck amplifying. Focus on the outcome you want—whether it's winning a specific game or simply increasing your chances of success.

5. Place the Clear Quartz: Hold the piece of clear quartz in your hand while concentrating on your intention. This stone will amplify the energy of the spell, helping you manifest your desires. Imagine the quartz glowing brighter with every breath, sending out waves of positive energy toward the game of chance.

6. Final Affirmation: Say aloud with confidence:

"The game is mine, luck's on my side, Victory's waiting, I'll not be denied. Fortune and success, I now embrace, Luck is my ally, in this sacred space."

7. Close the Ritual: Once you have finished the affirmation, leave the candles to burn down safely. Keep the coin and clear quartz with you as a reminder of your intent. You can carry the coin in your pocket or wallet, or keep it near where you will be playing the game.

Note: Stay positive and open to opportunities. The spell amplifies your natural luck, but remember that games of chance have an element of randomness, so trust the energy you've put out into the universe and let it flow toward you.

This simple yet powerful spell, performed on a Thursday during the Waning Moon, is a great way to increase your luck and give you the energy you need to succeed in games of chance.

06

SIMPLE AND POWERFUL MONEY SPELL FOR THE FIRST SUNDAY OF THE MONTH

The first Sunday of the month is an excellent time for setting intentions and attracting abundance for the upcoming weeks. Performing a money spell on this day aligns you with the energy of new beginnings and prosperity.

BEST DAY TO PERFORM THIS SPELL:

Sunday (Sun): Sunday is the day of the Sun, symbolizing vitality, success, and personal power. It's an ideal day to attract wealth and energize your financial goals for the upcoming month.

BEST MOON PHASE:

Waxing Moon: The Waxing Moon is the time when the moon is growing in strength, which is perfect for building wealth and manifesting financial growth. This phase is about attraction and expansion.

WHAT YOU'LL NEED:

- A green candle (for attracting money)
- A gold candle (for prosperity and abundance)
- A small bowl of honey (for sweetening your financial flow)
- A piece of paper and a pen
- A few coins (representing money flow)
- A small piece of cinnamon stick (for drawing money and prosperity)
- A comfortable, quiet space

INSTRUCTIONS:

1. Prepare Your Space: Find a quiet place where you can focus. Set the green candle on your left (to attract money) and the gold candle on your right (to enhance prosperity). Place the small bowl of honey in front of you as a symbol of sweetening your financial opportunities. Scatter a few coins around the candles and the bowl to represent the flow of money.

2. Set Your Intention: Sit in a comfortable position and take a few deep breaths. Close your eyes and visualize the kind of financial abundance you want to attract this month. See yourself surrounded by wealth, success, and opportunities that bring financial growth.

3. Light the Candles: Light the green candle first, saying:

"Money flows to me, abundance comes near, I draw wealth now, and I hold it here."

Then, light the gold candle, saying:

"Prosperity shines, I welcome the light, I embrace success with all of my might."

4. Write Your Intention: On the piece of paper, write down your financial goals for the month. Be specific and clear. For example:

"I attract $1,000 in new income this month through opportunities that come easily."

5. Anoint the Paper: Dab the paper with a little honey, symbolizing that the wealth and opportunities will flow easily and sweetly into your life. Fold the paper three times toward you, drawing the energy of abundance closer.

6. Add the Cinnamon Stick: Place the cinnamon stick on top of the folded paper to amplify the attraction of money and success. Cinnamon is known to speed up financial flow and make the energy of money work faster.

7. Hold the Coins: Hold the coins in your hand, visualizing them growing and multiplying. As you do, say:

"With every coin, my wealth grows, Opportunities come, the flow never slows."

8. Final Affirmation: Hold the folded paper, cinnamon stick, and coins together, and say aloud:

"On this Sunday, I set my intent, Money and success, I now represent. With this spell, my fortune will grow, The abundance I seek will surely flow."

9. Dispose of the Paper: Safely burn the paper or bury it to release your intention into the universe. Let the candles burn down completely, leaving you with the energy of abundance to carry through the month.

10. Close the Ritual: Keep the coins and cinnamon stick in your wallet, purse, or near your workspace as a reminder of the prosperity you're attracting. Carry the energy of the spell with you and stay open to the financial opportunities that the universe sends your way.

This simple and powerful money spell, performed on the first Sunday of the month during the Waxing Moon, helps you set the tone for abundance and financial success in the coming weeks.

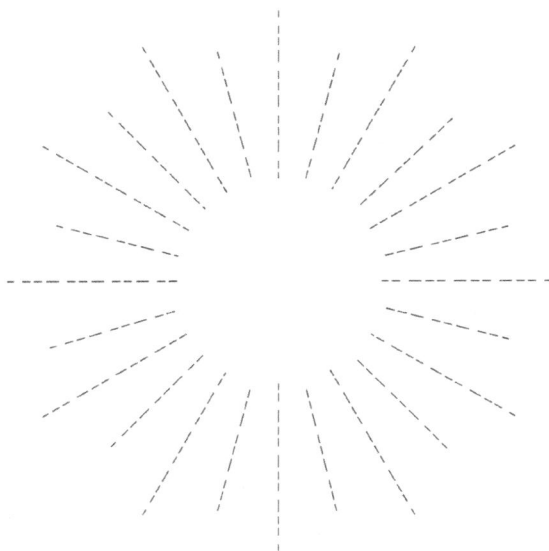

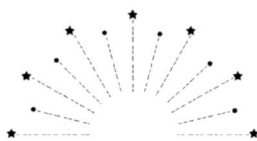

07

SIMPLE AND POWERFUL PROSPERITY BATH FOR QUICK ABUNDANCE

This prosperity bath is designed to cleanse your energy and invite financial success and abundance into your life. It combines the elements of nature with powerful herbs and oils to open the flow of prosperity quickly.

BEST TIME TO PERFORM THIS BATH:

Thursday (Jupiter): Thursday is the day of Jupiter, the planet of expansion and abundance, making it the best day to perform a prosperity bath to attract wealth and prosperity.

BEST MOON PHASE:

Waxing Moon: The Waxing Moon is ideal for bringing new opportunities, growth, and expansion, making it perfect for a prosperity ritual.

WHAT YOU'LL NEED:

- 1 cup of sea salt (for purification and protection)
- 1 tablespoon of cinnamon (for attraction and speed)
- 1 tablespoon of dried basil (for wealth and prosperity)

A few drops of essential oil:

- Citrus oil (such as orange or lemon) for success and freshness
- Patchouli oil for financial abundance
- A green candle (for prosperity) and a gold candle (for success)
- A comfortable, quiet space, preferably near a bathtub

INSTRUCTIONS:

1. Prepare Your Space: Clean your bathroom and prepare the bath. Light the green and gold candles near the bathtub to enhance the energy of the ritual and create a sacred space for prosperity. If you have time, take a few moments to clean your physical space as well, allowing it to be clear and open to new energy.

2. Prepare the Bath: Fill your bathtub with warm water, ensuring that it is at a comfortable temperature. As you do, sprinkle in the sea salt, allowing it to dissolve in the water. The salt will purify your energy and remove any negativity or blockages to your financial flow.

3. Add the Herbs and Oils: Add the dried basil and cinnamon to the bath. These herbs are known for their association with wealth, prosperity, and abundance. Drop in a few drops of your citrus oil and patchouli oil to attract fresh opportunities and amplify your financial abundance.

4. Set Your Intention: As the herbs and oils mix with the water, sit or stand near the bath and close your eyes. Take deep breaths and focus on what you want to bring into your life—whether it's new income, career growth, or financial freedom. Visualize abundance flowing into your life quickly and easily.

5. Immerse Yourself in the Bath: Slowly step into the bath, allowing the water to cleanse and soothe you. As you relax, imagine the water surrounding you with prosperity and abundance. Picture the money and opportunities you desire flowing toward you.

As you soak, say the following affirmation:

"Abundance surrounds me, prosperity flows, Wealth and success are mine to grow. Money and blessings come to me fast, I welcome them in, this bath will last."

6. Relax and Absorb the Energy: Soak in the bath for at least 1 5-20 minutes. Allow the herbs, oils, and energy to absorb into your skin and energy field. Feel yourself aligning with the flow of prosperity and abundance.

7. Close the Ritual: When you are ready to exit the bath, slowly drain the water. As it flows away, imagine the obstacles and negativity leaving your life with it. You are now open and ready to receive prosperity.

8. Final Affirmation: Once you've exited the bath, stand and say aloud:

"With this bath, I attract what I need, Prosperity and wealth, I shall succeed. Quick and easy, money will flow, This is my time, abundance will grow."

9. Dry Off and Carry the Energy: Dry off with a soft towel, imagining yourself being filled with prosperity and good fortune. Keep the candles burning until they burn out completely, allowing their energy to fully infuse the space.

This bath ritual, when performed on a Thursday during the Waxing Moon, is a powerful way to cleanse your energy, attract abundance, and ensure prosperity comes to you quickly. It works best when you feel open to receiving and are ready to take the necessary steps to manifest the wealth you desire.

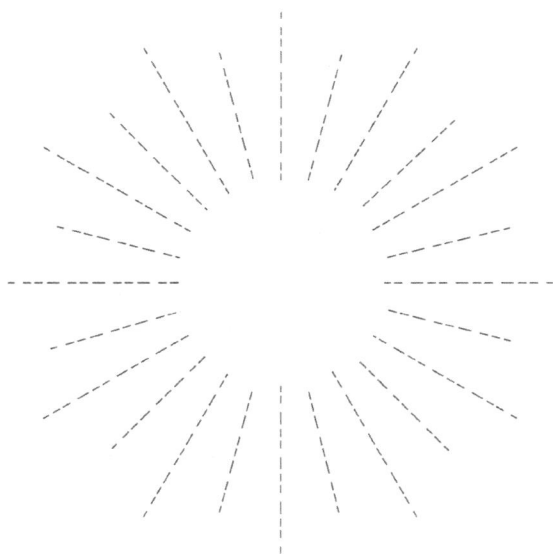

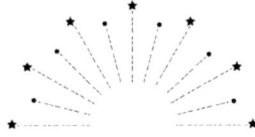

08

SIMPLE AND POWERFUL FOUR PENNY PAPA LEGBA MONEY SPELL FOR MONDAY

T his simple and powerful spell uses the energy of Papa Legba, the spirit of the crossroads, to open the roads to financial opportunities. The four pennies represent the four directions and the flow of money coming into your life. By performing this ritual on Monday, you align with the energy of new beginnings and growth.

BEST DAY TO PERFORM THIS SPELL:

Monday (Moon): Monday is ideal for starting new projects and inviting new opportunities. It's a day for cleansing, healing, and opening doors, making it perfect for money work.

WHAT YOU'LL NEED:

- 4 pennies (representing the four directions and the flow of money)
- A white candle (for invoking Papa Legba and spiritual guidance)
- A green candle (for prosperity and wealth)
- A small bowl of water (symbolizing fluidity and abundance)
- A small offering to Papa Legba (such as honey, rum, or tobacco)
- A piece of paper and a pen
- A comfortable, quiet space

INSTRUCTIONS:

1. Prepare Your Space: Set up your sacred space, preferably at a crossroads or an open area. Place the white candle to honor Papa Legba and the green candle for prosperity. Put the small bowl of water in the center as a symbol of abundance and fluid money flow.

2. Offer to Papa Legba: Place a small offering (such as a few drops of rum, a bit of honey, or tobacco) in front of the white candle to honor Papa Legba and invite him into your space. This offering is a gesture of respect to the spirit who opens doors and clears paths.

3. Arrange the Pennies: Place the 4 pennies in the four directions around the candles:

- **East (left):** Place the first penny, symbolizing new opportunities and the beginning of financial growth.

- **South (front):** Place the second penny, symbolizing the fast and steady flow of prosperity.

- **West (right):** Place the third penny, symbolizing the completion and fulfillment of your financial goals.

- **North (behind):** Place the fourth penny, representing the solid foundation and security of your wealth.

4. Write Your Intention: On the piece of paper, write down a clear and specific financial goal you wish to achieve. For example:

"Papa Legba, open the road to $1,000. Let it come quickly through unexpected opportunities."

5. Speak Your Prayer: Hold the piece of paper in your hands, stand in the center of your setup, and visualize the money flowing to you. As you focus on the pennies and your goal, say:

"Papa Legba, open the roads, To wealth and abundance, I now call. From East, South, West, and North, Let prosperity enter, and bring forth. Bless my path, clear the way, I welcome money without delay."

6. Light the Candles: Light the white candle to call Papa Legba's spirit and the green candle to call prosperity into your life. Let the flames burn for a while as you continue to visualize financial flow and abundance coming your way.

7. Seal the Energy: After a few minutes, take the piece of paper and fold it three times toward you. Place it under the pennies, then say:

"The roads are open, the path is clear, Money and wealth will soon appear."

8. Leave the Offering: Leave the offering to Papa Legba by the white candle as a thankyou gesture. Allow the candles to burn out naturally.

9. Close the Ritual: After the ritual, keep the four pennies in your wallet, purse, or somewhere safe where you keep your money, to continue attracting financial energy. The piece of paper can be kept in your wallet or altar as a reminder that the roads are open and prosperity is on its way.

Note: This ritual is simple yet powerful, focusing on honoring Papa Legba to open the roads for financial opportunities. The four pennies represent the flow of abundance, with each direction calling in prosperity from different angles. Perform this spell with faith, and trust that Papa Legba will guide you to financial blessings.

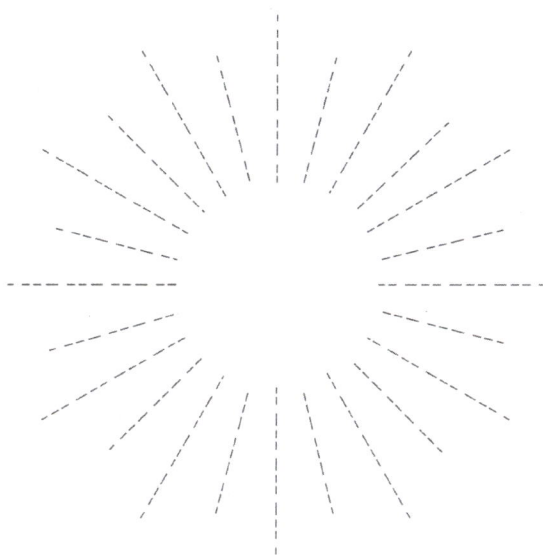

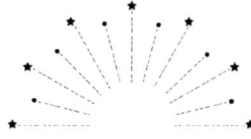

09

SIMPLE AND POWERFUL MONEY SPELL USING ORANGES AND MATCHES

This easy yet potent money spell utilizes oranges to symbolize abundance and the fresh flow of money, while matches are used to ignite the energy of your intentions. Oranges are known for their association with prosperity, and the act of lighting matches brings the energy of fire, activating the spell and infusing it with power.

BEST DAY TO PERFORM THIS SPELL:

Sunday (Sun): Sunday is a day of vitality, success, and achievement, making it a perfect day to perform a money spell to bring abundance into your life.

BEST MOON PHASE:

Waxing Moon: This phase is ideal for attracting and expanding financial opportunities.

WHAT YOU'LL NEED:

- 1 orange (symbolizing abundance and wealth)
- 3 matches (for activating and igniting your financial growth)
- A small piece of paper and pen
- A comfortable, quiet space
- A green candle (optional, to amplify prosperity energy)

INSTRUCTIONS:

1. Prepare Your Space: Set up a clean, quiet space where you can focus. If possible, light a green candle to further enhance the energy of prosperity, or place it on your altar. If you don't have a green candle, feel free to skip this step.

2. Write Your Intention: On the small piece of paper, write a specific amount of money or a financial goal you wish to manifest. For example:

"I attract $500 easily into my life through unexpected opportunities."

3. Prepare the Orange: Cut the orange in half. This symbolizes opening up the flow of abundance. As you cut the fruit, think about how the energy of wealth is now being made available to you.

4. Insert the Paper: Fold the piece of paper with your financial goal written on it three times toward you. Place it in the center of the orange, between the two halves. This will keep your intention within the fruit, channeling its energy toward attracting money.

5. Light the Matches: Take the three matches, one by one. As you light each match, say the following:

- **First Match:** "I light this flame to ignite wealth."
- **Second Match:** "This flame brings money to me."
- **Third Match:** "With this fire, abundance flows easily into my life."

Let each match burn for a few seconds before snuffing it out gently. Place the burnt matches on the orange or keep them in a safe place as a symbol of your spell's activation.

6. Place the Orange and Focus: Hold the orange in both hands and visualize the flow of money coming toward you. Picture the abundance filling your life—whether it's in the form of unexpected income, new opportunities, or financial growth. Imagine the orange absorbing and sending out this energy.

7. Final Affirmation: As you hold the orange, say aloud:

"With this orange, wealth I claim, Money and prosperity, I call your name. The road to riches is now clear, Abundance comes, I have no fear."

8. Allow the Orange to Sit: Leave the orange in a safe spot, preferably near your wallet, purse, or a place where you keep money, so that the energy of abundance can continue to build. Let the orange sit for at least a day or two, allowing the energy to marinate.

9. Dispose of the Orange: After a few days, when you feel the spell has had time to work, bury the orange outside or dispose of it in nature. This helps release the energy and allows the universe to manifest your financial intentions.

> **Note:** This is a very simple yet powerful spell that taps into the energy of nature and the elements (fire and abundance) to draw money toward you. Performing this ritual with focus and belief in its success will help you manifest prosperity more easily.

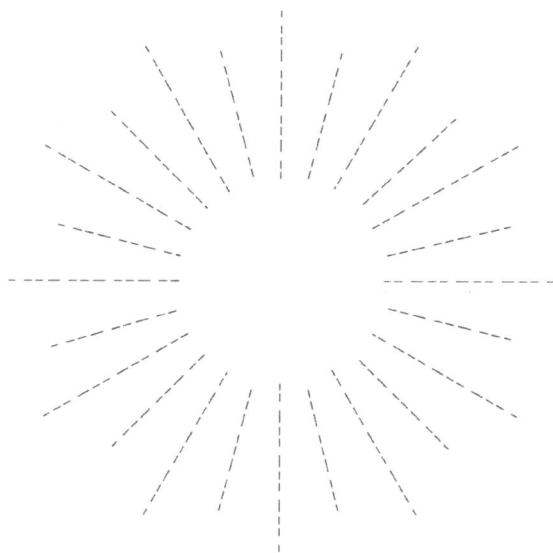

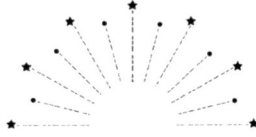

10
THE NEW YEAR HOME BLESSING SPELL

PURPOSE:

To cleanse, protect, and bless your home for a prosperous and harmonious year.

INGREDIENTS:

- A white candle (purity and divine light)
- A green candle (prosperity and growth)
- A small bowl of water (purification)
- Sea salt (cleansing and protection)
- Incense or sage (to remove negative energies)
- Olive oil or anointing oil (for blessings)

- A handful of dried herbs (rosemary for protection, basil for prosperity, lavender for peace)
- A bell or chime (to raise positive vibrations)
- A piece of paper and pen

STEPS:

1. Prepare Your Space
- Begin by tidying up your home. A clean space invites positive energy.
- Open your windows to allow old, stagnant energy to leave.

2. Create a Sacred Space
- Set up your candles, bowl of water, and herbs on a table or altar in the central area of your home.

3. Cleanse the Space
- Light the incense or sage and walk clockwise through each room of your home. As you do, say:

"I cleanse this space of all negativity. May only peace, love, and prosperity remain."

4. Bless the Water
- Sprinkle a pinch of sea salt into the bowl of water, saying:

"By earth and water, I cleanse and purify. May this water carry blessings into every corner of this home."

5. Anoint the Doorways

- Dip your fingers into the blessed water and lightly anoint doorways, windows, and mirrors. Say:

"May this home be protected, blessed, and filled with light throughout the coming year."

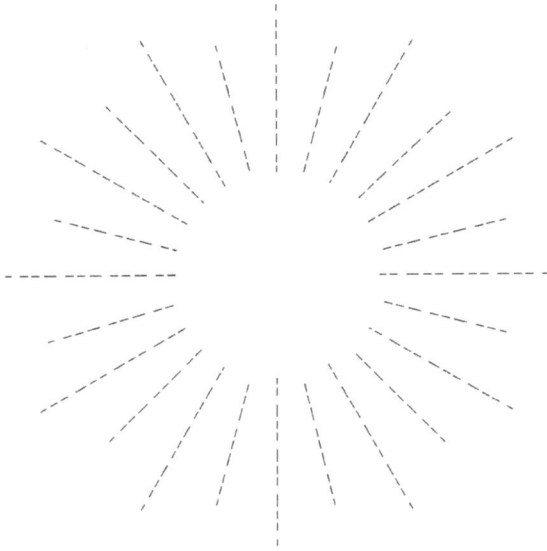

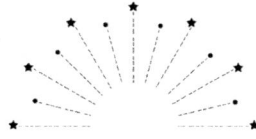

11

REMOVE EVIL EYE

EVIL EYE REMOVAL SPELL FOR SATURDAY

Purpose:

To break the influence of the evil eye, remove negativity, and shield yourself from future harm.

INGREDIENTS:

- A black candle (for banishment and protection)
- A white candle (for purity and cleansing)
- A bowl of water (for purification)
- Sea salt (to absorb negativity)
- Olive oil (blessed for protection)
- A piece of black obsidian or any protective crystal (optional)
- A sprig of rosemary or bay leaves
- (protection and cleansing)

- A needle, pin, or small sharp object (symbolic cutting of the curse)
- A mirror (to reflect and return negativity)

STEP ONE

1. Prepare Your Space
Choose a quiet, undisturbed area. Cleanse the space by burning sage, incense, or rosemary.

Place the candles, water, and other ingredients on a table or altar. Set the black candle on the left and the white candle on the right, with the bowl of water and salt in the center.

2. Ground Yourself
Sit comfortably and take deep breaths. Visualize a protective light surrounding you. Imagine any negative energy being drawn out of your body and replaced by pure, positive energy.

3. Set Your Intention
Say out loud:

> *"On this day of protection, I banish the evil eye cast upon me. Let it return to its source or dissolve into nothingness. I reclaim my energy and shield myself from harm."*

4. Light the Candles
Light the black candle, saying:

> *"I burn away all negativity, envy, and ill intent sent my way. As this flame burns, so does the evil eye vanish."*

Light the white candle, saying:

> *"I call upon light and purity to restore my energy and protect my spirit."*

5. Create a Cleansing Mix

Add three pinches of sea salt to the bowl of water, stirring clockwise. As you stir, say:

> *"By the power of earth and water, I cleanse myself of the evil eye. Let this water purify my spirit."*

6. Use the Mirror

Hold the mirror in front of you say:

> *"Mirror of truth, reflect all harm back to its source. Let the sender see their intent and let it harm no more."*

Place the mirror facing outward, toward the direction where you feel the negativity originated (if known).

7. Symbolically Cut the Curse

Take the needle or pin and pass it over your body (without touching your skin), as if cutting invisible threads. Say:

> *"I sever the ties of the evil eye. By this act, I am freed, and no harm can bind me."*

8. Cleanse Yourself with the Water

Dip your fingers into the salted water and lightly anoint your forehead, heart, and hands. Say:

> *"With this water, I wash away all malice and harm. I am cleansed, I am free, I am whole."*

9. Burn the Herbs

Light the rosemary or bay leaves and let the smoke surround you. As it burns, say:

"Protective flames, carry away all ill will and shield me from its return."

10. Seal the Spell

Extinguish the black candle first, saying:

"The darkness is banished and powerless."

Let the white candle burn until it extinguishes naturally, allowing the protective energy to grow.

11. Dispose of the Water and Salt

Pour the water outside, away from your home, and scatter any leftover salt in the wind.

TIMING:

Perform this spell on a Saturday evening, during a waning moon, for maximum banishing power.

> **Note:** Carry the protective crystal with you for extra shielding. Repeat the ritual weekly or monthly if you feel the evil eye's presence returning. Combine this spell with positive affirmations and daily protective practices.

May you be freed from all harm and shielded from negativity!

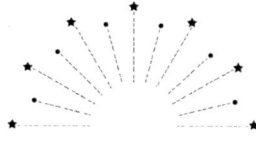

12
ARCHANGEL MICHAEL PROTECTION

Here's a powerful protection spell invoking Archangel Michael, the divine protector and warrior. This ritual calls upon his strength and light to shield you from harm, banish negativity, and create a sacred space of safety around you.

ARCHANGEL MICHAEL PROTECTION SPELL

Purpose:

To invoke Archangel Michael's divine protection, banish negativity, and create a shield of light around yourself or your home.

INGREDIENTS:

- A blue candle (symbolizing Archangel Michael's protective energy)
  Frankincense or sandalwood incense (to raise vibrations and purify the space)

- A small bowl of blessed water or holy water
- A sprig of rosemary or a protective crystal (e.g., black tourmaline or clear quartz)
- A white feather (optional, as a symbol of angelic presence)
- A piece of paper and pen

STEPS

1. Cleanse Your Space

Begin by lighting the incense and walking clockwise around your space, saying:

"I cleanse this space of all negativity. Only divine light and love may remain."

2. Create a Sacred Altar

Place the blue candle, bowl of water, rosemary or crystal, and feather on a table or altar. Arrange them in a way that feels meaningful to you.

3. Ground Yourself

Sit quietly, take a few deep breaths, and visualize roots growing from your feet into the earth, grounding you in stability and strength.

4. Light the Blue Candle

Light the blue candle and say:

"Archangel Michael, divine protector, I call upon you. Surround me with your heavenly light and shield me from all harm."

5. Pray for Protection

Hold your hands over your heart and recite this prayer with faith and intention:

"Archangel Michael, mighty guardian, Defender of truth and light, I ask for your protection this day and every night. Surround me with your sword of fire, Banish all harm and ill desire. Let no negativity touch my soul, Shield me with your love, make me whole. By your grace and divine power, Keep me safe every minute, every hour. Amen."

6. Bless Yourself with Water

Dip your fingers into the blessed water and anoint your forehead, heart, and hands, saying:

"With this water, I am purified and protected under Archangel Michael's watchful care."

7. Create a Shield of Light

Close your eyes and visualize a radiant blue light forming a protective sphere around you. Imagine Archangel Michael standing beside you, holding his fiery sword. Say:

"This shield of light, so strong and bright, Protects me day and night. By Archangel Michael's power divine, I am safe, I am free, all is fine."

8. Write Your Intention

On the piece of paper, write your specific request for protection *(e.g., "Protect me from harm," "Shield my home from negativity")*. Fold the paper and place it under the candle or crystal.

9. Close the Ritual
Thank Archangel Michael for his protection:

"Archangel Michael, I thank you for your presence and protection. May your light always guide and guard me. Amen."

Let the candle burn down safely (or extinguish it respectfully if needed).

10. Keep the Items Close
Place the rosemary, crystal, or feather near your bed, in your pocket, or at your front door as a symbol of Archangel Michael's ongoing protection.

TIMING:

Perform this ritual on a Sunday (a day of light and divine connection) or during a waxing moon to strengthen protective energies.

Note: Repeat this spell whenever you feel the need for extra protection. Maintain faith in Archangel Michael's power and presence, trusting that you are shielded and safe.

May Archangel Michael guard you with strength and divine light!

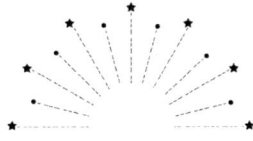

13

RETURN TO SENDER SPELL

Purpose:

To reflect negative energy, curses, or ill will back to its source, while shielding yourself from harm.

INGREDIENTS:

- A black candle (banishing and protection)
- A mirror (to reflect negativity)
- A small bowl of water
- Sea salt (for cleansing and protection)
- A sharp pin or needle (to symbolically cut ties)
- Sage, palo santo, or incense (to cleanse the space)
- A piece of paper and pen

STEPS

1. Cleanse Your Space
Burn sage, palo santo, or incense and walk through your space in a clockwise direction. Say:

"I cleanse this space of all negativity. Only light, love, and protection may remain."

2. Set Up Your Ritual Space
Place the black candle in front of the mirror. The mirror should face outward, symbolizing the reflection of harmful energy. Place the bowl of water with a pinch of sea salt near the candle.

3. Write the Source of Negativity
On the piece of paper, write the name of the person or situation you suspect is sending negative energy your way. If you're unsure, write:

"All negativity sent my way."

4. Light the Candle
Light the black candle and say:

"By this flame, I invoke protection and justice. All harmful energy sent to me is reflected back to its source."

5. Invoke Protection
Hold your hands over the bowl of salted water and say:

"Water of purity, salt of the earth, shield me from harm and cleanse my spirit. Surround me with your protective energy."

6. Use the Mirror

Hold the mirror in your hands and visualize all negative energy bouncing off of it and returning to its source. Say:

"Mirror of truth, reflect all harm. Return what was sent, with no added alarm. Let justice prevail, let harm dissolve, May peace and protection now resolve."

7. Cut the Energetic Ties

Use the pin or needle to symbolically cut ties to the negative energy. Pass the pin over the paper (without touching it), saying:

"I sever the ties of harm and ill will. This connection is broken, my spirit is still."

8. Burn the Paper

Carefully burn the piece of paper in a fireproof dish, visualizing the negativity dissolving into smoke. As it burns, say:

"As this paper turns to ash, so does all harm sent to me. It returns to its source, and I am free."

9. Extinguish the Candle

Snuff out the black candle, saying:

"This spell is complete. I am shielded, I am safe, I am whole."

10. Dispose of the Remnants

Pour the water and ashes outside, away from your home, and discard any remaining salt.

TIMING:

Perform this spell on a Saturday (associated with banishing and protection) or during a waning moon to release negative energy.

Note: Ensure your intentions are pure—this spell reflects energy but does not amplify harm.

Repeat if you feel negativity returning.

Practice daily shielding (visualizing a protective bubble of light around you) to maintain your protection.

May you be free from harm and surrounded by light and peace!

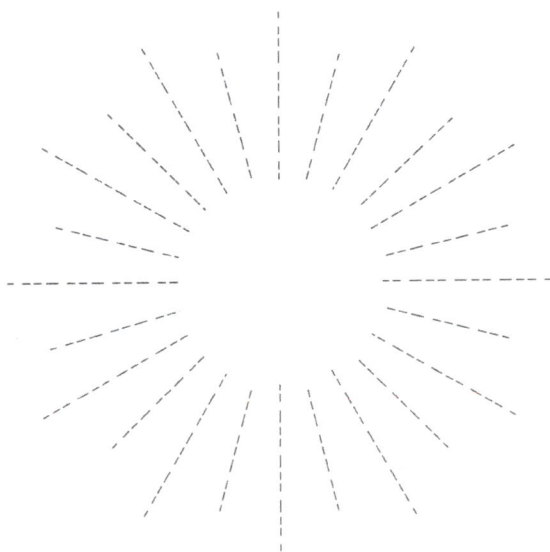

Made in the USA
Las Vegas, NV
08 March 2025

19099468R00033